INSTR...

HYMNS
& WORSHIP

Presents

The Stories Behind

Timeless
HYMNS

VOLUME ONE

By Dr. Steve Harney

INSTRUMENTAL HYMNS & WORSHIP

Table of Contents

Introduction

Welcome! I am thrilled that you have decided to take a few minutes out of your busy schedule to join me on a brief trip through time. We are going to take a journey through the ages and discover some intriguing stories and authors behind many Timeless Hymns.

We live in a day and age when contemporary songs and praise and worship music have risen to the forefront of many, if not most churches. There is nothing wrong with that, but as you will find in these stories, there is a rich heritage in these hymns that must never be forgotten. Many of them have touched hearts for hundreds of years, and for some very specific reasons. I am confident you will be blessed as we examine some of those reasons.

The first reason has to do with - the authors' life stories. Many of these hymns came out of great loss, sorrow, or costly devotion. Events were happening in people's lives that brought them to a point where the only way they could look was to God. A young man tragically loses his fiancé, starts his life over, and then tragically loses a second fiancé. What does he do? In his time of great loss, he turns to the Heavenly Father and writes about the deep friendship with God he has been able to develop during his time of grief. That is something we should all learn how to do.

The second reason is - the tremendous poetry portrayed in these hymns. Some of the greatest poetic lines of all time have been immortalized in hymns. Have you ever read the lyrics to Katharina von Schlegel's "Be Still My Soul?" Read these words slowly and let them sink in deeply.

> Be still, my soul: the Lord is on thy side.
> Bear patiently the cross of grief or pain;
> Leave to thy God to order and provide.
> In every change He faithful will remain.
> Be still, my soul: the best thy heav'nly Friend
> Thro' thorny ways leads to a joyful end.
> "Be still, my soul: thy God doth undertake
> To guide the future as He has the past.
> Thy hope, thy confidence let nothing shake;
> All now mysterious shall be bright at last.
> Be still, my soul: the waves and winds still know
> His voice who ruled them while He dwelt below.
> "Be still, my soul: the hour is hast'ning on
> When we shall be forever with the Lord,
> When disappointment, grief, and fear are gone,
> Sorrow forgot, love's purest joys restored.
> Be still, my soul: when change and tears are past,
> All safe and blessed we shall meet at last."

The third reason is the incorporation of - Christian doctrine. Singing hymns is one of the greatest ways to teach doctrine. You can do an entire sermon series on doctrine, but most people will not see the need to come and learn, it just sounds boring.   To say you are going to teach about theology generates a similar degree of excitement. But you can sing some of the great hymns and not only teach but the receivers will *learn* about the doctrines of the faith and why they are so important. Consider these two hymns as an example:

> God the Omnipotent
> O Love That Will Not Let Me Go

The titles alone speak volumes about who and what God truly is in our lives.

The final reason we will list today – is the hymns exalt and magnify the Lord Jesus Christ more than just about any other form of music. These are not songs that were written in order to fulfill a contract or project. They were not written to fill up the pages of a songbook. They were not written as part of a job to submit to those who were singing and recording songs. These hymns were written out of great tragedy, sorrow and emotional encounters. These writers were sharing how God had touched, moved and filled their hearts, souls, needs and lives.

Some of the verses were so personal that today we cannot sing those verses or stanzas. They would mean nothing to us, but to the writers they related how God had touched their very souls. They lifted up God by writing these hymns to tell the world how wonderful, loving and powerful a Holy awesome God truly is to each and every one of us.

I hope that as you read these stories you will realize that the hymns are a rich heritage for us all that will speak to our souls. Yes, we need praise and worship, it fires our emotions and thrills our hearts and souls. But we also need the hymns, for they challenge our hearts and minds, expand our understanding of God and remind us of our wonderful Christian heritage.

The Earliest Known Hymn

Did you know? In 1918 papyrologists Bernard Pyne Grenfell and Arthur Surridge Hunt were on an archeological dig in an ancient rubbish dump in Oxyrhynchus, Egypt. Along with codexes, edicts, tax-assessments, wills, leases, bills and more they found what has come to be called, *Oxyrhynchus 1786*, named for the town and the order in which it was discovered. Written at the end of the third century A.D., Oxyrhynchus 1786 is thought to be the oldest Christian hymn ever found. The lyrics are written in Greek and invoke one to silence for the praise of the Holy Trinity.

The music is written in Greek Vocal Notation and is diatonic, meaning it uses only the 8 note scale, no sharps or flats, the notes ranging from F to F above.

The Oxyrhynchus hymn is the only fragment of music we have left from the first 400 years of Christendom. The second oldest surviving hymn is the Sanctus melody from the Western medieval Requiem mass which dates from sometime in the 4th century.

The hymn has been featured in several modern recordings that have been included in a number of releases of Ancient Greek Christian music.

And to think of all of the things that were found in that rubbish dump, they found a hymn! The Scriptures tell us that we speak to ourselves and one another in psalms, hymns and spiritual songs (Eph. 5:19, Col 3:16). God has given us music to comfort our souls, soothe our hearts and brighten our days. It changes moods, pushes us forward and it reminds us of what God has done and will continue to do for us.

In the first century, Paul, under the inspiration of the Holy Spirit, told us what hymns could do. From this ancient, 3rd century, rubbish dump we find that the early church was busy singing hymns. Almost 2,000 years later, people still use that hymn, and countless thousands of others to speak to their souls. It is important, in this writer's opinion, that we do not forget those hymns today just because they don't have the cadence, timing or beat that we feel calls to a younger generation. Every song at one time was contemporary, but hymns have stood the test of time and can continue to make a difference in lives. History, and this hymn, prove that very fact.

So, remember this - never underestimate the power of a Hymn in your life. Not only do they each have a story, as we shall see in the pages to follow, but those stories and words can still speak to us today in ways, that for many, are beyond human belief.

Instrumental Hymns and Worship

Did you know? In 2020 the world seemed to fall apart - and so did many people. *What are we going to do? How are we going to survive? Where did all of this come from?* We were told to "shelter in place" and that we were "alone together." But that didn't stop one young man from dreaming.

Matt Fouch, bass singer for Dove Award winning southern gospel quartet, Legacy Five, decided there was more to do than just sit at home. So, he came up with an idea. "People enjoy listening to the old hymns and I enjoy listening to the old hymns, so…." With that thought in mind Matt - who can't play an instrument - created Instrumental Hymns and Worship. He found people who could play the old hymns, piano, guitar, bluegrass style, and more, and he started organizing them together in projects and genres. Today, thousands listen to these hymns everyday spurring memories from their childhood; of parents who have gone on; or simply enjoying sweet songs God gave to others to be a blessing to generations that would follow. Fanny Crosby, Robert Lowry, C A. Miles, Annie Hawks, people who never heard of a recording or radio, the internet or streaming - yet today, their songs live on thanks to all of these platforms. So, to Matt and all the others who make listening to these great old hymns possible, *Thank you!*

To listen to these great old hymns, check out www.instrumentalhymns.com

Matt Fouch

Tis So Sweet to Trust In Jesus

Did you know? Louisa Stead was born in Dover, England and was saved at the age of 9. Louisa came to the United States in 1871 and lived in the Cincinnati, OH area. She attended a camp meeting in Urbana, OH and surrendered her life to missionary service. But because of poor health she was unable to serve as a missionary at that time. Louisa married in 1875 and the couple had a baby, Lily. Hymnologist Kenneth Osbeck describes a major turning point in the family's life:

> "When the child was four years of age, the family decided one day to enjoy the sunny beach at Long Island Sound, New York. While eating their picnic lunch, they suddenly heard cries for help and spotted a drowning boy in the sea. Mr. Stead charged into the water. As often happens, however, the struggling boy pulled his rescuer under water with him, and both drowned before the terrified eyes of wife and daughter. Out of her 'why?' struggle with God during the ensuing days glowed these meaningful words from the soul of Louisa Stead."

> *'Tis so sweet to trust in Jesus,*
> *and to take him at his word;*

just to rest upon his promise,
and to know, "Thus saith the Lord."
Jesus, Jesus, how I trust him!
How I've proved him o'er and o'er!
Jesus, Jesus, precious Jesus!
O for grace to trust him more!

Stead later remarried and did become a missionary in South Africa. She eventually died in South Rhodesia, what is now modern-day Zimbabwe. It is said that following her death, Christians in South Rhodesia continued to sing her hymn in the local Shona language.

Louisa Stead (1850-1917)

'Tis So Sweet to Trust in Jesus

PROVERBS 30:5
Louisa M. R. Stead, 1882

William J. Kirkpatrick, 1882

1. 'Tis so sweet to trust in Je - sus, Just to take Him at His Word;
2. Oh, how sweet to trust in Je - sus, Just to trust His cleans - ing blood;
3. Yes, 'tis sweet to trust in Je - sus, Just from sin and self to cease;
4. I'm so glad I learned to trust Thee, Pre - cious Je - sus, Sav - ior, Friend;

Just to rest up - on His prom - ise, Just to know, "Thus saith the Lord!"
And in sim - ple faith to plunge me 'Neath the heal - ing, cleans - ing flood!
Just from Je - sus sim - ply tak - ing Life and rest, and joy and peace.
And I know that Thou art with me, Wilt be with me to the end.

Refrain

Je - sus, Je - sus, how I trust Him! How I've proved Him o'er and o'er;

Je - sus, Je - sus, pre - cious Je - sus! Oh, for grace to trust Him more!

Amazing Grace

Did you know? On Jan 1, 1773, an unknown preacher, at the time, wanted a poem to go along with his sermon for that day. As he began to write, these are the words that came to mind. "Amazing Grace, how sweet the sound, that saved a wretch like me." And so began a journey with a song that has been with us now for 250 years. That preacher, John Newton, was not only writing in regard to his text, 1 Chronicles 17:16-17, but he was also writing about his life. John Newton had once been the captain of a slave trading ship. Then, during a tremendous storm he cried out to God to save him, and God did. It was then that Mr. Newton came home, resigned his commission and started studying Christian Theology. He would go on to be ordained and pastor in Olney, England for many years. He would also become a huge abolitionist because of his newfound faith. His poem was put to more than 20 tunes throughout the years and was never very popular in England. But in the United States it became a staple. In 1835, William Walker set it to the tune we all know and love today. It is interesting to note that in the second verse, Rev. Newton records his own conversion. "'Twas grace that taught my heart to fear. And grace my fears relieved. How precious did that grace appear the hour I first believed." From a slave trader to a soul in need. From a soul in need to a Christian Pastor. From a Pastor to an avid abolitionist. Isn't it Amazing how Grace can change a heart for God?

John Newton (1725-1807)

Amazing Grace

John Newton

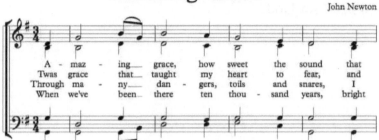

A - maz - ing grace, how sweet the sound that
Twas grace that taught my heart to fear, and
Through ma - ny dan - gers, toils and snares, I
When we've been there ten thou - sand years, bright

saved a wretch like me. I once was
grace my fears re - lieved; How pre - cious
have al - rea - dy come; Tis grace hath
shin - ing as the sun. We've no less

lost but now am found; was blind but now I see.
did that grace a - ppear the hour I first be - lieved.
brought me safe thus far and grace will lead me home.
days to sing God's praise than when we first be - gun.

Come Thou Fount

Did you know? Robert Robinson was born in Norfolk, England on Sept. 27, 1735, the only child of Michael and Mary Robinson. When he was 8 years old his father died. His maternal-grandfather, never having approved of his daughter's "lowly marriage" immediately dis-inherited his grandson. Therefore, as a young man, Robert had to begin acting as an adult and provide for he and his mother. At the age of 20 he was saved by the influence of the famous preacher, George Whitfield. Robert began his preparation for the ministry and soon became a Baptist Minister. It is said that at one time he pastored a church of over 1000 weekly attenders. Two years after his conversion he wrote this hymn.

Come Thou Fount of every blessing
Tune my heart to sing Thy grace;
Streams of mercy, never ceasing,
Call for songs of loudest praise
Teach me some melodious sonnet,
Sung by flaming tongues above.
Praise the mount! I'm fixed upon it,
Mount of God's unchanging love.

Later in his life, Rev. Robinson fell away from the Lord and found himself in a very deep depression. He was riding in a stagecoach one day, just he and a young lady. To break the monotony of the trip the young lady began to hum and sing, Come Thou Fount. When she had finished, she asked him what he thought of the hymn she was humming. He responded, "Madam, I am the poor unhappy man who wrote that hymn many years ago, and I would give a thousand worlds, if I had them, to enjoy the feelings I had then." Gently, she replied, "Sir, the 'streams of mercy' are still flowing." He was deeply touched by that. As a result of the encounter, he repented. His fellowship with the Lord was restored through the ministry of his own hymn, and a Christian's willing witness.

Robert Robinson (1735-1790)

Come, Thou Fount of Every Blessing
NETTLETON

Robert Robinson, 1758

Traditional American melody
John Wyeth's Repository of Sacred Music, Part Second 1813

1. Come, thou fount of ev-'ry bless-ing, tune my heart to sing thy grace: streams of mer-cy, nev-er ceas-ing, call for songs of loud-est praise. Teach me some me-lo-dious son-net, sung by flam-ing tongues a-bove; praise the mount! I'm fixed up-on it, mount of God's un-chang-ing love.

2. Here I raise my Eb-en-e-zer; hith-er by thy help I'm come; and I hope, by thy good plea-sure, safe-ly to ar-rive at home. Je-sus sought me when a strang-er, wan-d'ring from the fold of God; he, to res-cue me from dan-ger, in-ter-posed his pre-cious blood.

3. O to grace how great a debt-or dai-ly I'm con-strained to be; let that grace now, like a fet-ter, bind my wan-d'ring heart to thee. Prone to wan-der Lord I feel it-prone to leave the God I love; here's my heart, O take and seal it, seal it for thy courts a-bove.

Great is Thy Faithfulness

Did you know? Thomas Obediah Chisholm was born in Franklin, KY in 1866. He was educated in a simple country schoolhouse and at age 16 began teaching in that very same school. He became a Christian at age 27 and was ordained a Methodist minister at age 36. Chisholm spent most of his life in ill health. He eventually had to resign as a pastor and moved to Vineland, New Jersey where he opened an insurance office.

Chisholm wrote hundreds of poems but in 1923, while meditating on Lamentations 3:22-23 he wrote the text of Great is Thy Faithfulness. He sent this poem to his friend, William Runyan, and he wrote the music for Great is Thy Faithfulness.

But the story does not stop there. Runyan was friends with Dr. Will Houghton, the president of Moody Bible Institute. Runyan shared the song with Houghton and it became one of his favorites. Dr. Houghton then invited an unknown singer, George Beverly Shea to come and sing hymns on the Institute's radio station, and Shea included Great is Thy Faithfulness in his lineup.

But the story doesn't end there. A young man attending seminary, also in Chicago, at Wheaton College heard George Beverly Shea and loved the voice and the song. That young man, Billy Graham, would later invite Shea to come and be part of his evangelistic ministry and the song, Great is Thy

Faithfulness would be sung all over the world and gain worldwide appeal as a result.

Thomas Chisholm would spend most of his life in ill health and as a result made below average income all of his life. But he lived to be 94, passing away in 1960 in Ocean Grove, New Jersey. But his legacy in this one song still lives on today, because Great is God's Faithfulness.

Lamentations 3:22-23 [It is of] the LORD'S mercies that we are not consumed, because his compassions fail not. '[They are] new every morning: great [is] thy faithfulness.

Thomas Obediah Chisholm (1866-1960)

Great Is Thy Faithfulness

1 Great is thy faith-ful-ness, O God my Fa-ther, there is no
2 Sum-mer and win-ter, and spring-time and har-vest, sun, moon and
3 Par-don for sin and a peace that en-dur-eth, thy own dear

shad-ow of turn-ing with thee; thou chang-est not, thy com-
stars in their cours-es a-bove join with all na-ture in
pres-ence to cheer and to guide; strength for to-day and bright

pas-sions they fail not; as thou has been thou for-ev-er wilt be.
man-i-fold wit-ness to thy great faith-ful-ness, mer-cy and love.
hope for to-mor-row, bless-ings all mine, with ten thou-sand be-side!

Refrain

Great is thy faith-ful-ness! Great is thy faith-ful-ness!

Morn-ing by morn-ing new mer-cies I see; all I have need-ed thy

WORDS: Thomas O. Chisholm (1866-1960)
MUSIC: William M. Runyan (1870-1957)
Words and Music © 1923, Ren. 1951 Hope Publishing Company

FAITHFULNESS
11.10.11.10.Ref.

How Great Thou Art

Did you know? The year was 1885 and a young man in Sweden by the name of Carl Boberg had been to an afternoon church service. On his way home a thunderstorm rolled in. He and his friend quickly ran for cover. The lightning flashed across the sky, loud claps of thunder shook the hillsides and strong winds swept across the fields and meadows. But as soon as it had begun, the storm ended, blue skies appeared, and God's beautiful rainbow filled the sky.

Boberg went home and that evening sat down and began to write "O Store Gud" How Great Thou Art. The poem was later set to the tune of a Swedish folk song. In 1907, Manfred von Glehn translated the song into German, and in 1912 a Russian Pastor, Ivan Prokhanoff translated it into Russian.

In the 1920's Rev. And Mrs. Stuart K Hine left England and became missionaries in Poland. While there they took the Russian version and translated it into English. And thus began the song we now know as How Great Thou Art.

Sometime later J Edwin Orr introduced the English version to the United States. But it wasn't until 1957, during the New York City Crusades of Rev. Billy Graham, where it was sung 99 times, that the song truly began to travel the world and gained notoriety worldwide.

It has been almost 140 years since it was first written, but How Great Thou Art has become one of the top 100 most requested and favorite hymns of all time. And to think, it all started with a young man and a thunderstorm.

Carl Boberg (1859-1940)

Stewart K. Hine (1899-1989)

How Great Thou Art

In the Garden

Did you know? In March of 1912, in a cold, damp, dreary basement with no windows, and no view of a garden you would find C Austin Miles reading John 20:1-18. As he read, he visualized himself right there in the garden as Mary Magdalene first encountered her risen Savior. Jesus had revealed himself to her, but she hadn't recognized him. But then he called her by name, and immediately, Mary knew it was The Master. Isn't it amazing, when The Master calls your name, you always know that it is Him. With that passage and vision in mind, Mr Miles began to write, I come to the garden alone, while the dew, is still on the roses…. And the rest is history. However, there was some controversy with the song in the beginning. It was considered too erotic, by some publishers, because of the implied relationship between Mary and Jesus. Yes, you read that right. When you consider some of the songs that are published today, that seems laughable. However, the song was published in 1912 and was made popular in Billy Sunday Crusades all across America. It has been recorded by Roy Rogers and Dale Evans, by Tennessee Ernie Ford, Perry Como, Rosemary Clooney, Doris Day and even Elvis Presley. In later years it has been recorded by Willie Nelson, The Statler Brothers, Glenn Campbell and even Brad Paisley. What a tremendous legacy for a song written on the spur of the moment in a dark, dreary basement on a cold March morning as C Austin Miles became the onlooker to that first meeting of Mary and her risen Savior.

Charles Austin Miles (1868-1946)

In the Garden

1. I come to the gar - den a - lone,
2. He speaks, and the sound of His voice
3. I'd stay in the gar - den with Him,

while the
is so
though the

dew is still on the ros - es; and the voice I hear fall - ing
sweet the birds hush their sing - ing; and the mel - o - dy that He
night a - round me be fall - ing; but He bids me go; through the

on my ear, the Son of God dis - clos - es.
gave to me with - in my heart is ring - ing. And He walks with me, and He
voice of woe, His voice to me is call - ing.

talks with me, and He tells me I am His own, and the

joy we share as we tar - ry there, none oth-er has ev-er known.

WORDS: C. Austin Miles, 1912 (John 20:11-18)
MUSIC: C. Austin Miles, 1912

GARDEN
8.9.5.5.7 with refrain

It Is Well with My Soul

Did you know that there is more to the story than you have probably heard. Almost all of us have heard the story of the wealthy lawyer, and modern-day Job, Horatio G Spafford, who had a very successful real estate business in Chicago. But in the year 1871, everything began to change. First his four-year-old son died of scarlet fever in 1871. Shortly thereafter, the great Chicago fire destroyed almost all of his real estate investments which destroyed his fortune. But Mr. Spafford began to work hard once again, and by 1873, through wise decisions, had regained a fair amount of his wealth.

He decided that his family needed a much-deserved rest and being close friends with D.L. Moody and Ira Sankey, he decided his family needed time away. So, the decision was made to go to England to help their friends with their evangelistic efforts and at the same time, get some much-needed rest. However, at the last minute, Mr Spafford had to send his family on without him as he had to stay behind and finish some last-minute financial business. Just four days into the trip his wife and four daughters would once again experience devastation. Their ship, the S.S. Ville du Havre, was struck by the iron English ship, Lochearn, and sunk in 12 minutes. Mrs. Spafford told of gathering her four daughters, ages 12, 7, 4 and 18 months, on the deck of the ship and praying that God would spare them and if not, that they would accept His will. Within minutes the ship had sunk, and Mrs. Spafford was found clinging to a piece of wood, alone. She was rescued, taken to Wales where she telegraphed her husband, "Saved Alone. What shall I do?"

Horatio took the next ship and immediately headed to be with his grieving wife. The captain called Horatio, four days into the trip, telling him that they were very near the site where his daughters perished. His daughter Bertha, born in 1878, would later tell how her father returned to his cabin and there wrote the words to It is Well. Later Phillip P. Bliss would set the words to music and the rest, as they say, is history.

But - did you know - Horatio named his poem, It is Well with my soul. Which is very interesting. Why? The name of the ship his wife and daughters were traveling on, was the S.S. Ville du Havre. If you translate that into English you get, The City of Haven. Or literally, A place that is well and safe.

And when Phillip Bliss wrote the tune for the song, he named the tune, Ville du Havre, the Safe Place.

You see, Horatio G. Spafford had a safe haven, a place that was well. He was in the arms of his Savior. And if God be for me, who can be against me.

Horatio Gates Spafford (1828-1888)

It Is Well with My Soul

VILLE DU HAVRE

Horatio G. Spafford, 1873

Philip P. Bliss, 1876

1. When peace, like a riv-er at-tend-eth my way, When sor-rows like sea-bil-lows roll; What-ev-er my lot, Thou hast taught me to say, "It is well, it is well with my soul."

2. Though Sa-tan should buf-fet, tho' tri-als should come, Let this blest as-sur-ance con-trol, That Christ has re-gard-ed my help-less es-state, And hath shed His own blood for my soul.

3. My sin - O the bliss of this glo-ri-ous thought, My sin - not in part but the whole, Is nailed to the cross and I bear it no more, Praise the Lord, praise the Lord, O my soul!

4. And, Lord, haste the day when the faith shall be sight, The clouds be rolled back as a scroll, The trump shall re-sound and the Lord shall de-scend, "E-ven so" - It is well with my soul.

It is well_____ with my soul,_____ It is well, it is well with my soul.

It is well It is well with my

Just As I Am

Did you know? Charlotte Elliot was born in Claphan, England in 1789, one of six children. Her grandfather was a preacher and one of those considered to be instrumental in the Great Awakening of the 18th century in England. Charlotte lived in Claphan for the first 32 years of her life. Highly educated and gifted in art and humorous verse, she was most welcomed at social events of the day where religion was not mentioned or at least was not center stage.

However, in 1821, at age 32, she suffered a serious illness which removed her from these social settings and for the most part left her weak and an invalid for the rest of her life. In 1822 a well-known preacher, Dr. Caesar Malan of Geneva, Switzerland visited her and asked a very important question, "Charlotte, are you at peace with God?" Charlotte resented the question and refused to talk to Dr. Malan that day.

But a few days later she sent for him and apologized for her behavior. She then explained that she wanted to clean up her life before coming to the Savior. To this Dr. Malan replied, "Come just as you are." That day, May 9, 1822, Charlotte committed her life to Christ.

Twelve years later, thinking back to that day and her conversation with Dr. Malan, she began to write:
Just as I am - without one plea,

But that Thy blood was shed for me,
And that Thou bidst me come to Thee,
-O Lamb of God, I come!
William B Bradbury composed the music and published the song in 1849. It has been translated into many languages and has been used in more altar calls than any other hymn in history. Dr. Billy Graham wrote that his team used this hymn in almost every one of their crusades because it presented "the strongest possible Biblical basis for the call of Christ."

Charlotte Elliot (1789-1871)

Just as I Am, without One Plea

814

1 Just as I am, with-out one plea but that thy
2 Just as I am, and wait-ing not to rid my
3 Just as I am, though tossed a-bout with man-y a
4 Just as I am, poor, wretch-ed, blind, sight, rich-es,

blood was shed for me and that thou bidd'st me come to
soul of one dark blot, to thee, whose blood can cleanse each
con-flict, man-y a doubt, fight-ings and fears with-in, with-
heal-ing of the mind, yea, all I need, in thee to

thee, O Lamb of God, I come, I come.
spot, O Lamb of God, I come, I come.
out, O Lamb of God, I come, I come.
find, O Lamb of God, I come, I come.

5 Just as I am, thou wilt receive,
   wilt welcome, pardon, cleanse, relieve;
   because thy promise I believe,
      O Lamb of God, I come, I come.

6 Just as I am; thy love unknown
   has broken ev'ry barrier down;
   now to be thine, yea thine alone,
      O Lamb of God, I come, I come.

Sweet Hour of Prayer

Did you know? Sweet Hour of Prayer, a longtime favorite hymn of the church was first penned in 1842 by William Wolford, an obscure, blind lay preacher who served in Coleshill, England, in the mid-19th century. He owned a small trinket shop in the village. His poem was later given to William Bradbury who composed music for so many beloved gospel hymns such as "Just As I Am" (Charlotte Elliott), "The Solid Rock" (Edward Mote) and "He Leadeth Me" (Joseph H. Gilmore). Bradbury wrote the music for this favorite hymn in 1861 and first published it in his collection Golden Chains, from which it has become a staple of hymnals around the world. Whether you are a blind owner of a trinket shop, President of the United States of America or Jesus Christ, the Son of God, we all need to spend more time in that Sweet Hour of Prayer, on our knees before the Father!

There is no known picture of William Walford. Some are not even sure he is the author of the poem. He cannot be truly traced. There is a Rev. William Walford who served as President of Homerton Academy, which would have been about 110 miles from Coleshill. He authored a book, the Manner of Prayer which follows a lot of the thoughts of the hymn. However, he was not blind and did not own a trinket shop. What we do know is that William B

Bradbury did write the music hymn and he is pictured below.

William B Bradbury (1816-1868)

Sweet Hour of Prayer

1. Sweet hour of prayer, sweet hour of prayer, that calls me from a world of care and bids me at my Fa-ther's throne make all my wants and wish-es known! In sea-sons of dis-tress and grief, my soul has of-ten found re-lief, and

2. Sweet hour of prayer, sweet hour of prayer, thy wings shall my pe-ti-tion bear to Him whose truth and faith-ful-ness en-gage the wait-ing soul to bless; and since He bids me seek His face, be-lieve His word and trust His grace, I'll

3. Sweet hour of prayer, sweet hour of prayer, may I thy con-so-la-tion share, till, from Mount Pis-gah's loft-y height, I view my home and take my flight. This robe of flesh I'll drop and rise to seize the ev-er-last-ing prize; and

WORDS: William Walford, 1845
MUSIC: William B. Bradbury, 1861

SWEET HOUR
LMD

There is a Fountain Filled with Blood

Did you know? William Cowper (pronounced Cooper) was born in Great Berkhampstead, England on Nov. 26, 1731. His father was a chaplain and his mother passed away when William was just 6 years old. Cowper was sent to boarding schools, and it was while attending one of these that he first began to experience emotional difficulties.

After graduating he was apprenticed to a solicitor (lawyer). He was eventually called to the Bar but never practiced law. He was later nominated to the Clerkship of Journals of the House of Lords. However, as he was being interviewed for the position, he experienced an anxiety attack and was not appointed to the position. This led to a state of deep depression in Cowper's life.

He was treated at St Alban's Hospital and while there resided with Rev. Morley Unwin. His depression slowly lifted, and Cowper developed a lifetime friendship with Unwin's wife.

Unwin passed away in 1767, and John Newton, author of Amazing Grace, invited Unwin's wife and family along with Cowper to move to Olney where he pastored a small church. While there Newton and Cowper became very close friends and started a publication called The Olney Hymns.

During this time, and while in depression, Cowper wrote his most famous and controversial hymn, There Is A Fountain Filled With Blood.

Based on Zechariah 13:1, "On that day a fountain shall be opened for the house of David and the inhabitants of Jerusalem, to cleanse them from sin and impurity," the hymn is a meditation on the saving power of the blood of Christ.

Many have tried to revise it and make it less graphic, but the fact still remains, "without the shedding of blood there is no remission." (Heb 9:22). Cowper himself made a few revisions, over the years, but most of those were to simply make the song more personal to the believer in general and less about just Cowper himself.

William Cowper (1731-1800)

There Is a Fountain Filled with Blood

William Cowper, 1731 - 1800

American melody
Arr. by James T. Barth

Trust and Obey

Did you know? It was 1886 and D.L. Moody was holding one of his famous revivals in the city of Brockton, Massachusetts. Daniel B. Towner was leading the music that week and Ira D. Sankey was the special guest singer. Sankey, in his biography, My Life and the Story of the Gospel Hymns gives this account of what took place one night.

"Mr. Moody was conducting a series of meetings in Brockton, Massachusetts, and I had the pleasure of singing for him there. One night a young man rose in a testimony meeting and said, 'I am not quite sure—but I am going to trust, and I am going to obey.' I just jotted that sentence down and sent it with a little story to the Rev. J. H. Sammis, a Presbyterian minister. He wrote the hymn, and the tune was born."

Sammis is said to have immediately jotted down the lines to the refrain after reading the letter and adding the verses a little later. Towner would place the words to music, and within a year, 1887, the hymn would be published in the collection, Hymns Old and New. Since that time, it has been published in countless hymnals around the world.

Some say the hymn is based on 1 John 1:7 and others say it is I Samuel 15:22. There is no clear evidence either way. But what is clear, is this,
"…there's no other way, to be happy in Jesus, but to Trust and Obey!

Rev. John H. Sammis (1846-1919)

Now you are the light in the Lord. Live as children of light. Ephesians 5:8

1. When we walk with the Lord In the light of His Word, What a glo - ry He
2. Not a shad - ow can rise, Not a cloud in the skies, But His smile quick - ly
3. Not a bur - den we bear, Not a sor - row we share, But our toil He doth
4. But we nev - er can prove The de - lights of His love Un - til all on the
5. Then in fel - low-ship sweet We will sit at His feet, Or we'll walk by His

sheds on our way! While we do His good will, He a - bides with us still,
drives it a - way; Not a doubt nor a fear, Not a sigh nor a tear
rich - ly re - pay; Not a grief nor a loss, Not a frown nor a cross
al - tar we lay; For the fa - vor He shows And the joy He be - stows
side in the way; What He says we will do, Where He sends we will go;

Refrain

And with all who will trust and o - bey.
Can a - bide while we trust and o - bey.
But is blest if we trust and o - bey. Trust and o - bey, For there's
Are for them who will trust and o - bey.
Nev - er fear, on - ly trust and o - bey.

no oth - er way To be hap - py in Je - sus, But to trust and o - bey.

TEXT: John H. Sammis
MUSIC: Daniel B. Towner

TRUST AND OBEY
6.6.9.D. with Refrain

What a Friend We Have in Jesus

Did you know? In 1844 a young Irishman, Joseph Scriven, had completed his college education and was returning home to marry his sweetheart. As he was traveling to meet her on the day before the wedding, he came upon a horrible scene - his beautiful fiancée tragically lying under the water in a creek bed after having fallen off her horse. Devastated, Scriven moved to Canada and eventually fell in love again, only to experience devastation once more when she became ill and died just weeks before their marriage.

The following year, he wrote a poem to his mother in Ireland that described the deep friendship with Jesus he had cultivated in prayer through the hardships of his life. In 1868, attorney Charles Converse set that poem to a tune and renamed it "What a Friend We Have in Jesus."

Instead of thinking God was punishing him, Scriven cherished God's friendship through all of this hardship - a friendship he discovered in prayer. May we learn that our relationship with God will grow the same way - in prayer.

Joseph Scriven (1819-1886)

What a Friend We Have in Jesus

1. What a friend we have in Je - sus, All our sins and griefs to bear!
2. Have we tri - als and temp-ta - tions? Is there trou-ble an - y-where?
3. Are we weak and heav - y lad - en, Cum-bered with a load of care?

What a priv - i - lege to car - ry Ev - 'ry-thing to God in prayer!
We should nev - er be dis-cour-aged— Take it to the Lord in prayer!
Pre - cious Sav-ior, still our ref - uge— Take it to the Lord in prayer!

Oh, what peace we of - ten for - feit; Oh, what need-less pain we bear
Can we find a friend so faith - ful Who will all our sor-rows share?
Do thy friends de-spise, for-sake thee? Take it to the Lord in prayer!

All be-cause we do not car - ry Ev - 'ry-thing to God in prayer.
Je - sus knows our ev - 'ry weak-ness— Take it to the Lord in prayer!
In His arms He'll take and shield thee— Thou wilt find a sol-ace there.

Blessed Assurance

Did you know? Fanny Crosby, America's most prolific hymn writer, wrote 8,000 Gospel songs and hymns during a lifetime, which spanned nearly a century. She passed away in her 95th year. All of her days, except the first six weeks, were spent in blindness. She would later become known as Aunt Fanny.

One day in 1873, Aunt Fanny was visiting with a friend, Mrs. Joseph Knapp, a musician of sorts and wife of the founder of Metropolitan Life Insurance Company. During their visit Mrs. Knapp played a tune on her piano, which she had recently written. She then asked Fanny, "What does this tune say?" After kneeling in prayer for a few moments, she rose and declared, "It says, 'Blessed assurance, Jesus is mine!'" Aunt Fanny began to dictate verses to Mrs. Knapp, who wrote them down, fitting them to the melody just as we hear it sung today.
Blessed assurance, Jesus is mine
Oh, What a foretaste, of glory divine
Heir of salvation, purchase of God
Born of his spirit, Washed in his blood.

Did you also know that Fanny Crosby and Bing Crosby were related? It is distant, but they are related.

Frances Jane Crosby (1820-1915)

473

Blessed Assurance

Acts 17:30-31; Rev. 7:9-14

Fanny Crosby, 1873; alt.

1 Bless-ed as - sur - ance, Je - sus is mine! O what a
2 Per - fect sub - mis - sion, per - fect de - light! Vi - sions of
3 Per - fect sub - mis - sion, all is at rest, I in my

fore - taste of glo - ry di - vine! Heir of sal - va - tion, pur - chase of
rap - ture now burst on my sight; An - gels de - scend - ing, bring from a -
Sav - ior am hap - py and blessed; Watch-ing and wait - ing, look - ing a -

God, born of the Spir - it, washed in Christ's blood.
bove ech - oes of mer - cy, whis - pers of love.
bove, filled with God's good - ness, lost in Christ's love.

Refrain

This is my sto - ry, this is my song, prais-ing my Sav-ior all the day long;

After hearing Phoebe Knapp play this tune on the piano, Fanny
Crosby composed the poem on the spot. In her almost 95 years,
Crosby wrote more than 8,500 gospel hymns and songs.

Tune: ASSURANCE Irr.
Phoebe P. Knapp, 1873

I Am Thine O Lord

Did you know that Fanny Crosby was not born blind, she was blinded at 6 weeks of age when she developed an eye infection, and a mustard-based ointment was applied to her eyes which damaged her optic nerve leaving her blind for life. Also, she is known as Fanny Crosby or Aunt Fanny in the US, but in all British hymnals she is known by her married name, Frances Van Alstyne.

Fanny wrote 8000 - 9000 hymns depending on who you read, but she was not a composer. So, she would write the words, but others wrote the music. Fanny worked with such great Christian composers as William Bradbury, William Doane, Robert Lowry and Ira Sankey.

The hymn, I Am Thine O Lord, came to be as Crosby and William Doane were sitting and talking one evening about the nearness of God in their lives. When Fanny went to her room that night her mind was flooded with the ideas and words from their conversation that evening. As she lay in her bed that night, we formed the lines of "I Am Thine O Lord" before falling asleep that evening. When she awoke the next morning, she quoted the words to Doane who wrote down the stanzas and composed the tune.

The year was 1874, and the hymn was composed in Cincinnati, OH where Crosby was visiting with William Doane and other personal friends.

Fanny and her husband Alexander van Alstyne

156. I am Thine, O Lord.

Draw me nearer. 10, 7, 10, 7. With Chorus.   WILLIAM H. DOANE.

1. I am Thine, O Lord, I have heard Thy voice, And it told Thy
2. Con - se - crate me now to Thy serv - ice, Lord, By the pow'r of
3. Oh, the pure de - light of a sin - gle hour That be - fore Thy
4. There are depths of love that I can - not know Till I cross the

love to me; But I long to rise in the arms of faith,
grace di - vine; Let my soul look up with a stead-fast hope,
throne I spend, When I kneel in prayer, and with Thee, my God,
nar - row sea; There are heights of joy that I may not reach,

REFRAIN.

And be clos - er drawn to Thee.
And my will be lost in Thine. Draw me near - er,
I com - mune as friend with friend. near - er, near - er,
Till I rest in peace with Thee.

near - er, bless - ed Lord, To the cross where Thou hast died; Draw me

near-er, near-er, near-er, bless-ed Lord, To Thy pre-cious, bleeding side.

FANNY J. CROSBY.

I Need Thee Every Hour

Did you know? Annie Sherwood Hawks began writing hymns at age 14. She wrote about 400 hymns and poems, but I Need Thee Every Hour is the only one we still sing today. After she got married in 1859, she gave up most of her writings to take care of her husband, three children and home. She was a member of Hanson Place Baptist Church in Brooklyn, NY where her pastor was Robert Lowry, the famed hymn writer and composer of the 19th century.

In 1872, at the age of 37, here are Annie's own words to describe how this hymn came to be. "I was busy with my regular household tasks during a bright June morning. Suddenly, I became so filled with the sense of nearness to the Master that, wondering how one could live without Him, either in joy or pain, these words were ushered into my mind, the thought at once taking full possession of me -- 'I Need Thee Every Hour. . . .'"

Her pastor wrote the music and added the refrain to what we all now know and love, I need Thee Every Hour.

Annie Sherwood Hawks (1836-1918)

404   I Need Thee Every Hour

1. I need Thee ev-ery hour, most gra - cious Lord;
2. I need Thee ev-ery hour, stay Thou near - by;
3. I need Thee ev-ery hour, in joy or pain;
4. I need Thee ev-ery hour, teach me Thy will;
5. I need Thee ev-ery hour, most Ho - ly One;

no ten - der voice like Thine can peace af - ford.
temp - ta - tions lose their power when Thou art nigh.
come quick - ly and a - bide, or life is vain.
Thy prom - is - es so rich in me ful - fill.
O make me Thine in - deed, Thou bless - ed Son.

I need Thee, O I need Thee; ev - ery hour I need Thee!

O bless me now, my Sav - ior, I come to Thee.

WORDS: Annie S. Hawks, 1872
MUSIC: Robert Lowry, 1872

NEED
6.4.6.4 with refrain

I Surrender All

Did you know? Judson Van DeVenter was an accomplished musician and he worked as an art teacher in the local public school in the town where he lived. He was actively involved in his church and in evangelistic meetings around the area. In the late 1880's some of DeVenter's friends encouraged him to become an evangelist and follow his true calling. DeVenter left teaching and surrendered to be an evangelist. He wrote this account of his decision.

"The song was written while I was conducting a meeting at East Palestine, Ohio... For some time, I had struggled between developing my talents in the field of art and going into full-time evangelistic work. At last, the pivotal hour of my life came, and I surrendered all. A new day was ushered into my life. I became an evangelist and discovered down deep in my soul a talent hitherto unknown to me. God had hidden a song in my heart, and touching a tender chord, he caused me to sing."

He wrote the song in 1890, it was later put to music and published in 1896. In this short little song, the one who sings all five stanzas will sing the word "surrender" thirty times. The other key word – "all" –

will be sung forty-three times! And all five stanzas
begin with the phrase, All to Jesus I surrender.

Judson Van DeVenter (1855-1939)

I Surrender All

Judson W. Van DeVenter

Winfield S. Weeden

1. All to Je - sus I sur - ren - der, All to Him I free - ly give;
2. All to Je - sus I sur - ren - der, Make me, Sa - vior, whol - ly Thine;
3. All to Je - sus I sur - ren - der, Lord, I give my - self to Thee;

I will e - ver love and trust Him, In His pre - sence dai - ly live.
Let me feel Thy Ho - ly Spi - rit, Tru - ly know that Thou art mine.
Fill me with Thy love and po - wer, Let Thy bles - sing fall on me.

I sur - ren - der all, I sur - ren - der all;
I sur - ren - der all, I sur - ren - der all;

All to Thee, my bless - ed Sav - ior I sur - ren - der all.

Jesus Loves Me

Did you know? Anna B Warner wrote Jesus Loves Me This I Know originally as a poem for a novel, Say and Seal, written by her sister, Susan Warner, in 1860. But what many don't know is this. The sisters lost their mother at an early age. Their father, who was a successful New York attorney, lost everything in the financial crash of 1837. They subsequently lost their home and were forced to move to an old farmhouse in West Point near the United States Military Academy.

This is where the sisters began their work. They never married, wrote many novels and Anna wrote many songs and hymns. The sisters held regular Bible studies for the cadets, Anna wrote a new hymn each month for her Sunday School class and sharing the love of Jesus Christ became their life's mission.

The popularity of Jesus Loves me was so huge that both sisters were buried with military honors at West Point Cemetery, the only civilians given such honor, due to their contribution to the spiritual health of the soldiers. What an amazing story of two little girls from New York, with a love for Jesus and a passion to tell others about Him!

Anna B Warner (1827-1915)

Jesus Loves Me

584

1 Je - sus loves me! This I know, for the Bi - ble tells me so.
2 Je - sus loves me! He who died heav-en's gates to o - pen wide.

Lit - tle ones to him be - long; they are weak, but he is strong.
He will wash a - way my sin, let his lit - tle child come in.

Refrain

Yes, Je - sus loves me! Yes, Je - sus loves me!

Yes, Je - sus loves me! The Bi - ble tells me so.

Jesus Paid It All

Did you know - It was a hot, sultry Sunday morning in 1865. Elvina Hall was sitting in the choir loft in her usual place at the Monument Methodist Episcopal Church in Baltimore, MD. The pastor was speaking and as he did Elvina's mind began to wonder. She thought about the meaning of the cross, our need for salvation and all that God had done for her and every other Christian. Suddenly it was as if the song began to write itself.

Elvina had no paper to on which to write, so she began to pen her notes on the fly leaf of the hymnal in her hand.

"Jesus paid it all. All to Him, I owe.
Sin had left a crimson stain.
He washed it white as snow.
When before the throne
I stand in him complete.
Jesus died my soul to save.
My lips shall still repeat."

After the service she showed the notes to her pastor. Just that week the church organist had shared some music with the pastor, and he thought the tune and words would work well together. He put Elvina and the organist together. Elvina had written 4 verses but no chorus. The organist had written a chorus, but no verses. The two fit perfectly together and the rest as they say is history.

There is no known picture of Elvina M Hall. She was born in 1820 and she passed away in 1889.

Jesus Paid It All 276

Leaning on the Everlasting Arms

Did you know that Anthony Showalter and Elisha Hoffman wrote Leaning on the Everlasting arms together. Hoffman wrote the stanzas and Showalter wrote the refrain and the music.

Showalter was a musician who conducted music schools. He studied music in England, France and Germany and was an Elder at the First Presbyterian Church in Dalton, GA. The refrain for Leaning on the Everlasting Arms came about as a result of an epiphany of the verse Deuteronomy 33:27, "The eternal God is thy refuge, and underneath are the everlasting arms". Showalter learned that two of his former music students' wives had died and were buried on the same day. In a letter or sympathy to these two young men he created this refrain.

> Leaning, leaning,
> Safe and secure from all alarms.
> Leaning, leaning,
> Leaning on the everlasting arms.

He then asked Hoffman, a composer of over 2000 compositions and compiler of more than 50 different song books, to write the stanzas, then Showalter added the music. The rest as they say, "Is history."

Anthony Johnson Showalter (1858-1924)

Leaning On The Everlasting Arms

lisha A. Hoffman

Anthony J. Showalter

Softly and Tenderly

Did you know? There is no heart pounding, tear jerking story behind the hymn Softly and Tenderly. If anything, there is more of a lesson of perseverance and determination. Even when others reject you, keep pressing on. Sounds like something else I have heard. How does that go? "Lean not on your own understanding and He shall direct your paths." Yes, that's it!

Softly and Tenderly, Jesus is calling (as it was originally titled) was written by Will Lamartine Thompson. Will was a composer of gospel, secular and patriotic songs. Due to his songs being rejected, Will decided to form his own publishing company. Softly and Tenderly was first published in a collection of Thompson's songs entitled Sparkling Gems Nos 1 and 2 and quickly became a very popular hymn and was soon incorporated into many church hymnals.

Will Thompson devoted himself to writing songs after attending a meeting by a popular evangelist of the day, D. L. Moody. They became good friends in life, and when Moody was dying, he said to Thompson, "Will I would rather have written Softly and Tenderly Jesus is Calling than anything I have been able to do in my whole life."

Softly and Tenderly has been recorded by many artists through the years, Reba McEntire, Trisha Yearwood, Johnny Cash, Alan Jackson and The Cathedral Quartet just to name a few. It is one of the most popular invitational hymns ever written.

Will Lamartine Thompson (1847-1909)

Softly and Tenderly Jesus Is Calling

1. Soft - ly and ten - der - ly Je - sus is call - ing, call - ing for
2. Why should we tar - ry when Je - sus is plead - ing, plead - ing for
3. Oh, for the won - der - ful love he has prom - ised, prom - ised for

you and for me. See, on the por - tals he's wait - ing and watch - ing,
you and for me? Why should we lin - ger and heed not his mer - cies,
you and for me! Though we have sinned, he has mer - cy and par - don,

Refrain

watch - ing for you and for me.
mer - cies for you and for me? "Come home, come home!
par - don for you and for me. Come home, come home!

You who are wea - ry, come home." Ear - nest - ly, ten - der - ly,

Je - sus is call - ing, call - ing, "O sin - ner, come home!"

The Old Rugged Cross

Did you know that the popular hymn "Old Rugged Cross" was written in 1912? Methodist evangelist George Bennard wrote the country gospel favorite as he traveled to revival meetings. In the fall of 1912, Bennard finally wrote the first verse, which was apparently a response to the sneering comments he had received at a revival meeting in Albion, Michigan. Before the year ended and with a renewed meaning of the cross etched in his mind and heart. Bernard traveled from Chicago to Sturgeon Bay, Wisconsin, where they held evangelistic meetings, and the song eventually took shape in bits and pieces.

The completed song was first published in 1915. From this point, "Old Rugged Cross" became a staple at evangelistic crusades. It then proved to be an extremely popular country gospel song when it was recorded by numerous artists. This includes Ernest Tubb who used it as the title track of his 1952 gospel album. Other popular artists who covered the song are Merle Haggard, Johnny Cash, George Jones, Patsy Cline, and many more.

Rev. George Bennard (1873-1958)

The Old Rugged Cross

63

George Bennard, b. 1873   George Bennard, b. 1873

1. On a hill far a-way stood an old rug-ged cross, The em-blem of
2. Oh, that old rug-ged cross, so de-spised by the world, Has a won-drous at-
3. In the old rug-ged cross, stained with blood so di-vine, A won - drous
4. To the old rug-ged cross I will ev - er be true, Its shame and re-

suf-fering and shame; And I love that old cross where the dear-est and best
trac-tion for me; For the dear Lamb of God left His glo-ry a-bove
beau-ty I see; For 'twas on that old cross Je-sus suf-fered and died
proach glad-ly bear; Then He'll call me some day to my home far a-way,

REFRAIN

For a world of lost sin-ners was slain.
To bear it to dark Cal-va-ry.   So I'll cher-ish the old rug-ged
To par-don and sanc-ti-fy me.
Where His glo-ry for-ev-er I'll share.   cross, the

cross,........ Till my tro-phies at last I lay down; I will cling to the
old rug-ged cross,

old rug-ged cross,......... And ex-change it some day for a crown.
cross, the old rug-ged cross,

What a Day That Will Be

Did you know? The year was 1955 and James Hill had never written a song in his life. Yet as he sat and reflected that day, two things kept coming to his mind. First, he had heard a young, orphaned girl sing at church years earlier, and when she finished her song she said, "What a day that will be." The second thought in James' mind was about his mother-in-law. She had been paralyzed by a stroke at age 50. James was a new Christian and was wrestling with how this could happen to such a wonderful woman. As James sat there that day, this song began to write itself. He taught it to his wife and sister-in-law. It wasn't long until they went to visit his mother-in-law, and all the way there they practiced the song. Once they arrived, they sang the song for her. For the first time in 3 years, James' mother-in-law smiled and showed signs of excitement.

James took this to mean that God had his hand upon this song. And apparently, He truly did. Since then, this song has become an anthem of help, encouragement and strength to literally thousands of people. The song has been recorded by over 1000 different groups and individuals.

Revelation 21:4 And God shall wipe away all tears from their eyes; and there shall be no more death, neither sorrow, nor crying, neither shall there be any more pain: for the former things are passed away.

Jim Hill (1930-2018)

Hymn Stories from Friends

Greg Hamilton - Christian Magician
Favorite Hymn: *What a Day That Will Be*
The words of this hymn give us something to look forward to. During the good times and the not so good times.

Susan Hamilton - Retired School Teacher
Favorite Hymn: *I Surrender All*

When there are times in your life, that you worry about things, you just have to surrender them all to God.

Joey Cosme – Pastor, Bulakan, Philippines
Favorite Hymn: *He Lives*

The song "He lives" has impacted my life since I was in the Bible school. Every time I face trials, discouragement and downfall in my Christian life

I am always reminded that I serve a risen Savior and He lives within my heart. It became my favorite song and has been my encouragement to keep pressing forward.

Chuck Rathel - Retired Pastor
Favorite Hymn: *It Is Well With My Soul*

Growing up in a home with a mother who was a Marine D.I. (Drill Instructor), and a father who was a thirty-year senior Pilot in the Air Force, was almost beyond belief.

As a child, we went through the Korean War and Vietnam Conflict with countless other traumatic military events sprinkled along the way.

I have often pondered, as a second grader in Japan, being in the middle of the 1952 bloody May Day riot in downtown Tokyo where our car was about to be rolled into the mote around the Emperor's Palace with us in it by a crowd too big to number.

Living on an Air Force base in Japan during the Korean War I remember the many nights the air raid siren would go off and we would be bombed by the enemy who had somehow found a plane and flown it under the radar to the base to blow up airplanes parked just 100 feet from my house. To say my young life was filled with traumatic events that I have struggled a lifetime to understand is putting it mildly. There has been one hymn that has impacted my life like no other. The hymn, "It Is Well With My Soul" is about the peace God can bring in the midst of incomprehensible struggles.

I studied those traumatic events in the life of Horatio Spafford and wept at the loss of all of his children but found a calming peace for those storms in my life through his response to those events.

The God Horatio Spafford loved, served, and trusted is my God. In the hymn, "It Is Well With My Soul" proclaiming his complete confidence in God let me know it is well with my soul also.

Gary Longstaff – Pastor, Springfield, MO
Favorite Hymn: *Victory In Jesus*

I've tried to pick a favorite stanza but each one speaks to me at various times.

I love the reference to the "old old story" and the stanza of His healing "and somehow Jesus came to me and brought the victory"

Jo Moody - Single Women's Ministry, Beaumont, TX
Favorite Hymn: *Just as I Am*

My dad used to love to belt this out at the top of his lungs and tell me that the thief on the cross next to Jesus went as is with Jesus to "Paradise" THAT VERY DAY! He was not told to hop off the cross, get his life right, and come back. No! All he had to do was believe Jesus was whom He said he was—faith! Because of that, that thief entered paradise THAT DAY! I came to understand much more about that song even after my salvation. I didn't have to dust myself off before I could approach Him, He was still calling me to draw near, even on the days I blew it. He still does!!

Mike Davis - Pastor, Farmersville, KY
Favorite Hymn: *How Great Thou Art*

This Hymn is undoubtedly my favorite hymn. Every day, I look to the Lord in awesome wonder because He created a beautiful world in which to live, and He allowed a sinner like me to be saved. When I personally encountered God the first time, I was an alcoholic single father who had been raised in an unchurched home. I had no direction and no hope, and my daughters had a grim future before them, but God gave me hope. I was blessed to encounter Him in a church where I was saved, met my wife, watched my family grow, and surrendered to the call to preach the gospel. God spent no expense in giving me a gift I did not, and still do not, deserve... Jesus Christ! I regularly think of all He has done in my life, and I am overwhelmed by His greatness. Yet, as great as He is, God took the time to assure me, one child of millions, that one day He will send Jesus back for me! These are the main reasons why *How Great Thou Art* is my favorite hymn. It is a hymn that never gets old, nor can it! In my opinion it is not only the greatest hymn about the greatness of God, but it is one of the best hymns in presenting the gospel of Jesus Christ! I am overwhelmed with the greatness of God every time I sing it!

Brenda McCants - Retired Office Worker
Favorite Hymn: *Tell Me The Story of Jesus*

I love the tune of it, and I love the words. It literally brightens my world every time we sing it.
Ron Abbott - Retired Pastor
Favorite Hymn: *I've Anchored My Soul In The Haven Of Rest*

When I pastored in Bowie, Texas I was known to burst into song while strolling through the fellowship hall. Church folks eventually stopped being shocked at this and just smiled. This was one of my favorite songs to sing while strolling.

Mike Span – Pastor, Gulfport, MS
Favorite Hymn: *Come and Dine*

Lately I find myself humming this hymn all the time. It reminds me that my Master is calling me to spend time with Him. I can feast at His table any and all the time if I want. But I know He calls me regularly to spend time with Him in His Word and in prayer. Every time I do I come away encouraged, strengthened, and hopeful because my Lord is with me every step of the way!

Walt Yeomans – Pastor, Chesaning, MI
Favorite Hymn: *Victory in Jesus*

I have enjoyed this hymn throughout my journey as a child of God. I remember singing it in church services as a young teen. It always amazed me that God loved me, a little nobody, to the place that He saved me. He uses me in His work even today, some 50 plus years later! Verse one says"I heard an old, old story how a Savior came from glory, How He gave His life on Calvary to save a wretch like me: I heard about His groaning, of His precious bloods atoning, Then I repented of my sins and WON THE VICTORY! That's what He did for me. Thanking the Lord every day for what He has done for me.

Leny Funtecha - Filipino Missionary to Haiti and the Dominican Republic
Favorite Hymn: *No One Ever Cared For Me Like Jesus*

I grew up in a Christian family, but my father died when I was a month old. In short, I grow up very spoiled. After high school my family encouraged me to go to Bible school but I refused and took a secular course instead. After a couple of years I went to one of the southern islands in the Philippines to look for a job. One of my cousins had traveled with me and promised to help me find a good paying job. Before he left to return home, he pointed out a little church not far from our rented apartment and encouraged me to go. It was Wednesday so I attended the church service. That night a young girl sang a beautiful song

"No one ever care for me like Jesus". I was touched and for the first time I truly received Jesus Christ as my savior. I never did find a good paying job while I was there, but praise God I found my Savior. Truly he cares for me.

Mike Harmon – Retired Pastor
Favorite Hymn: *O Zion Haste*

I first heard of this song *O Zion Haste* in 1978 while on deputation raising my support for our ministry in Brazil. The words of this song tell us that it is our highest call, to proclaim the gospel to all nations, to all people, telling the world about the huge need of a personal Savior. We are not only to tell, but to send those to regions beyond, places that we cannot go ourselves. Our message of salvation can never change, it is the utmost importance that we tell the good news, Jesus Saves. Lives for eternity are at stake, may we pour out our soul in prayer victorious! Reaching people with the gospel, is truly the heartbeat of our Mission!

End Notes

All stories, resources and authors were confirmed at the sites listed below.

www.en.wikipedia.org
www.umcdiscipleship.org
www.hymnololyarchive.com
www.hymnary.org
www.christianmusicandhymns.com
https://www.azquotes.com/quotes/topics/hymns.html

INSTRUMENTAL
HYMNS
& WORSHIP

26157423R00050